BASICS

URBAN ANALYSIS

\\ GERRIT SCHWALBACH

BASICS

URBAN ANALYSIS

BIRKHÄUSER
BASEL · BOSTON · BERLIN

CONTENTS

FOREWORD

Studying existing urban structures, with their diverse social, historical and architectural influences, is a major part of modern urban planning. Cities and city districts are often marked by many generations, each with a different way of thinking. An urban neighborhood is characterized by the way these many influences overlap.

Analyzing the mechanisms behind an urban neighborhood's characteristics, recording its broader spatial context, and identifying the failings and mistakes of urban planning form the basis for safeguarding the long-term future of existing urban neighborhoods and their further development. This makes city analysis fundamental to any urban planning project. It is also the basis for intelligent urban planning context handling when implementing actual construction projects.

The *Basics* books on urban planning provide a basic grounding and various practical working methods for students of urban planning and architecture. Supplementing *Basics Urban Building Blocks*, an introduction to individual urban structural elements, the subject of this book is the analysis of existing urban structures and their characteristics. The emphasis is on explaining how to prepare and implement analyses of all urban factors, deal with sources of data and information and work in a specific area of analysis. The author presents methods of analysis from his own practical experience, demonstrates analysis result documentation types and reviews possible courses of action based on these results. *Basics Urban Analysis* is a valuable combination of methodical approaches and practical knowledge that students will find useful both academically and professionally.

Bert Bielefeld
Editor

INTRODUCTION

Urban planning always demands analysis of the area involved. This provides the background knowledge and rationale for any urban planning measure. Urban analysis, the study of existing urban spaces, is the preliminary stage of urban planning in any existing city.

Urban planning has increasingly less to do with quantitative growth and more to do with caring for and adapting existing urban structures, especially in Europe. This change in orientation requires intensive study of existing urban structures. The fundamental question, however, is whether existing cities' future development can actually be planned, and whether this kind of development can be determined in advance by analyzing the initial conditions. > Fig. 1

Urban planning has been determining future demands on urban spaces by measuring particular values for a long time. This approach

Fig.1:
Town planning within organic urban structures requires a thorough urban analysis.

intensified with the coming of the 20th century. During the Industrial Revolution, many cities experienced almost totally unplanned expansion. Experts noted their functional deficiencies. The planning approach developed as a response was particularly strongly represented in the 1960s, as the emergence of computers enabled extensive data processing and made advance planning of urban development with precision look like a realizable goal. The role of the urban planner also changed, with the unaccountable master builder becoming a rational engineer who would diagnose the city and then prescribe developmental planning measures. However, all efforts to precisely predetermine a city's development failed. Today, urban development processes are considered far too complex and contradictory to be understood and extrapolated in their entirety. Despite this realization, urban planning and urban analysis remain indispensable, but they are not used to plan every detail of urban development. Instead, they provide a basis for integrating diverse individual developments into a single planning scheme. With urban planning increasingly focusing on existing infrastructure, urban analysis has a key role. Before a need for action can be discovered and appropriate stabilization measures can be put in place, existing urban structures must be analyzed. Urban analysis does not precede urban planning in a fixed, self-contained process; rather, they are both elements in a continuous process. › Fig. 2

Urban analysis Urban analysis describes or analyses particular factors relevant to urban planning, in whole cities or in smaller areas within cities. Aesthetic, spatial, social or economic factors are recorded and represented in the study, which goes on to describe the interactions between these effects – which, however, cannot be assessed or described in full because the city and its users interact in a reciprocal system. Urban analysis is therefore confined to abstract, model interpretations of the city or its individual areas. › Fig. 3

Cities are generally perceived in a very different way by different parties. Factors like the emotional ties of residents to their neighborhood or their place in the local society of a certain neighborhood are incomprehensible to outsiders. Conversely, faults in urban design etc. may be of only minor importance to local residents. The urban planning process regularly involves serious conflict between urban planners and residents or users of the city due to their different perceptions and evaluations of a city. Initial conflicts are unavoidable, but if handled properly they represent a chance to develop a deeper understanding of the situation within the space under observation, spurring residents to look beyond the context of their own neighborhood and giving urban planners an insight into that neighborhood's social mechanisms. › Fig. 4

Fig.2:
Many individual developments come together in an organic urban structure.

Fig.3:
Urban analyses do not reproduce a city in its entirety.

11

Fig.4:
Cities can be perceived in very different ways.

Urban analysis may be part of a formal planning process. In the context of public development programs or urban renovation or renewal, an urban analysis may be implemented according to specific requirements. In general, however, the implementation of an urban analysis is not standardized; i.e. its extent and degree of detail must be decided based on the individual situation.

THEORETICAL PRINCIPLES OF URBAN ANALYSIS

A city can be represented as a tangible, perceptible spatial phenomenon, without precisely analyzing or describing its causative factors. Conversely, a city can be seen as the field of activity for scientifically measurable factors, without reference to its spatial dimension. Spatial analyses generally avoid both of these extreme approaches, instead describing a city as an interaction of different effects, but all with spatial implications. The main reference point is usually the perceptible city – urban analysis cannot exist without reference to tangible, perceptible phenomena.

AESTHETIC OBSERVATION: THE VISIBLE CITY

> ◊

A major part of urban analysis is the visual perception of a city; i.e. the recording and interpretation of visually perceived urban structures. We generally perceive a city without recognizing the mechanisms of perception, yet the task of describing a city is inseparable from the act of perceiving it.

Perception is a learned communication process. In this context, perception means the understanding of visual information. We can only understand phenomena that we have already perceived. This involves generalizing from one or more recurring characteristics, previously learned by and therefore known to the viewer. Individual characteristics may vary or change over time, but the general characteristics must remain constant for the phenomenon to be recognized.

Communication structures our environment. When we accept names for things, we are unconsciously using a pattern to perceive our surroundings. This is also a condition for being able to perceive. In this sense, the human sensory organs do not transport all stimuli to the brain. Instead, like a filter, they classify, selecting from the full range of available sensory stimuli in a data-compression operation.

◊
\\ Note:
Aesthetics (from the Greek aísthesis: perception) originally meant the study of beauty. Aesthetics in the scientific sense includes all mechanisms of human perception.

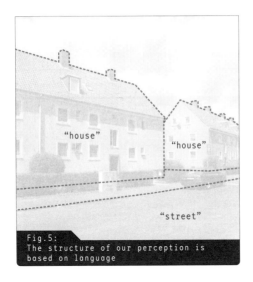

Fig.5:
The structure of our perception is
based on language

The process of determining names and terms is not learned discretely, but is inscribed into a culture in the form of language and perpetuated by the collective memory. The structure of our perception is based upon language. Language-based categories determine the differences (a selection process) and connections (a construction process) that we perceive, evaluate and interpret in our surroundings. This is largely an unconscious process, making it difficult for us to believe that different people perceive their surroundings differently, depending on their experience and habits.
> Fig. 5

Many of the terms we use group together very different urban features into a single category. This is like the way we perceive a human face. Rather than remembering all the individual features, what we notice is the overall impression created by the combination of those features. In a similar way, when we perceive a city, we compare it to many patterns with which we are familiar. We expect a town square, a historical church or town hall in the center of a city, for instance. In actual fact, this cognitive pattern is an idealized composite seldom seen in reality, where town centers are made up of many different phenomena, but we use our standard, familiar pattern to pick up on those parts of the overall composition that conform to the schema. Those parts that do not fit the pattern are suppressed by the perception process. If these elements form the dominant impression, then we do not perceive the city center, for instance, as being a city center. > Figs 6 and 7

Fig.6:
When we perceive a city, we compare it with the patterns we already know.

It follows that we recognize only those phenomena that can be abstracted, based on what we already know. Or, to put it another way, we perceive only the phenomena we expect. As perception is a cultural phenomenon, urban structures may be perceived very differently by people with different cultural backgrounds.

Urban analysis may confirm familiar perception patterns by underscoring certain phenomena as being particularly typical. However, it can also help people to recognize new phenomena or connections by explaining the rules governing perception.

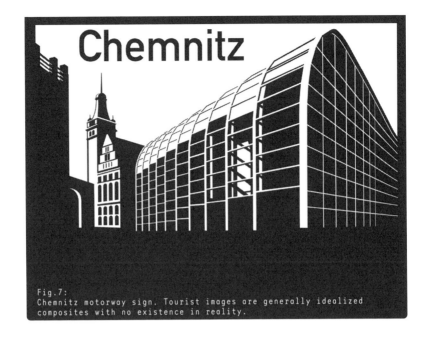

Fig.7:
Chemnitz motorway sign. Tourist images are generally idealized composites with no existence in reality.

SCIENTIFIC OBSERVATION: THE INVISIBLE CITY

A host of individual phenomena interact to produce our aesthetic perception of a city. Scientific methods, on the other hand, analyze individual aspects, with no claim to providing a general explanation of the city as a phenomenon. The smaller the area under consideration is, the more precisely it can be described. Scientists use this method to explain phenomena that lie outside the structure of perception or are not perceptible by the senses. While perception unites factors in an overall impression, science deconstructs the overall impression to discover the individual factors. For instance, characteristics of a district can be traced back to demographic features of its population without these phenomena being tangibly perceptible. › Fig. 8

Defined values Scientific urban analysis is based on assessing and interpreting defined values. The resulting measurements are usually interpreted by comparing them with measurements from other survey areas or timeframes. Analyzing statistics, such as the age or employment status of the population, is a typical example. The interaction of all active values in an urban space cannot be scientifically investigated. Individual aspects, however, can be described precisely, as exact measurements and comparative values are available.

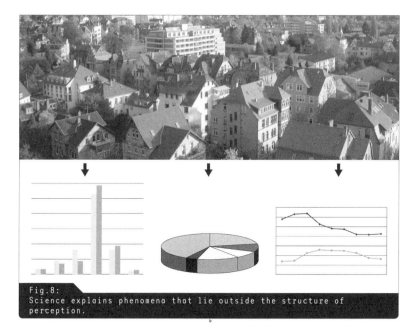

Fig.8:
Science explains phenomena that lie outside the structure of perception.

INTEGRATIVE OBSERVATION: THE LOGICAL CITY
Morphological description

Urban morphology describes the spatial characteristics of city structures and explains the conditions and causes behind them, including, for instance, the cultural, political or topographic context. Urban morphology, therefore, often follows a cause-and-effect pattern, with particular circumstances creating specific spatial structures.

Urban morphology involves intensive study of historical urban ground plans, i.e. the distribution of streets and building plots, usually based on a fundamental distinction between planned and non-planned or organic cities. Other criteria include the density and distribution of the buildings, the situation and hierarchy of streets and squares, the proportion of open spaces to built-up areas, and the placement of significant

\\ Note:
Morphology is the science of shapes and forms.
Urban morphology describes the form of cities
and residential estates and their processes of
formation.

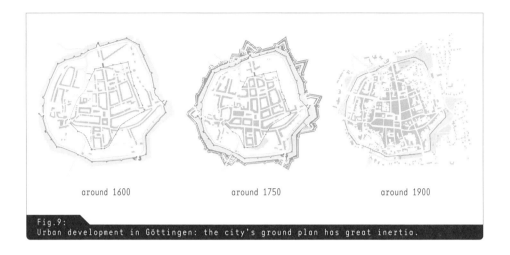

around 1600   around 1750   around 1900

Fig.9:
Urban development in Göttingen: the city's ground plan has great inertia.

buildings in the city's ground plan. Individual structural features are often studied, including:

_ Development structure: individual buildings, block buildings and rows
_ Access structure: streets, commons, squares and bridges
_ Open space structure: open space and bodies of water

While individual buildings have a comparatively short lifespan, the ground plans of cities are generally very slow to change. Street plots in particular possess great inertia. Historical cities therefore contain the traces of many different eras. While street plans often date from the founding of the city, most buildings will have been replaced or modified many times, so that the remains of many different eras, all of which arose under different circumstances, are jumbled together within a city. This means that morphological urban analysis may provide many explanations within a single city. > Fig. 9

\\ Note:
Analysis of urban morphology can reveal the logic of an area by investigating the conditions and causes of its characteristics.

Fig.10:
Construction styles can help us work out the age of a building.

Analysis of building style

Analysis of building style compares the formal composition of buildings and urban structures from different eras (historical styles), regions (regional styles), or cultural movements. In rare cases, individual architects or municipal building officers originate a style that characterizes a city. Style is always created by the culturally active minority, so that rather than being urban space's primary shaping force it is an intellectual, formal expression of traditional building experience.

The study of style does not necessarily explain the cause of each style. Even so, particular worldviews or construction technologies can help to elucidate a style, giving the subject applications beyond "decoration".

Analyzing styles often helps us to work out the age of buildings or urban structures. Not every era, however, has its own distinctive style. Often, several different styles were used simultaneously, or there were long transitional phases between stylistic eras. Determining style and date of origin is often made more difficult by the redesign of historical buildings and changes to the city's ground plan, so that stylistic analysis often relies on detailed historical analysis. › Fig. 10

Analysis of functional patterns

Most methods of analysis describe urban structures as a consequence of other circumstances, reasoning that social, climatic, economic or cultural conditions bring about particular spatial urban structures.

Fig.11:
Even if designs differ …

Fig.12:
… the functional pattern of a building
entrance is readable to all visitors.

Analysis of functional patterns assumes that this works both ways: as well as social and cultural activities creating spatial structures, spatial structures have implications for social and cultural behavior. One might say that spatial structures act as a catalyst for the social activities of the urban space's users.

Readability
of spatial
structures
We are not born knowing the social behavior appropriate to given spatial structures. It is learned, like a language, and is tied to a cultural context. Any changes to spatial structures must therefore preserve their readability if the relationship between place and behavior is not to be disrupted.

One of the key functional pattern schemas of a city designates public and private spaces. A varied repertoire of spatial structural characteristics encodes public or private city space. For instance, a square with a central monument encircled by shops declares itself to be public. › Figs 11 and 12

The association between social behavior patterns and certain spatial structures are very long-lived, but even so, new functional patterns can arise. New functional patterns usually arise by analogy with already familiar systems.

Functional patterns may be tied to particular social or cultural milieus, so that spatial codes can only be read by members of a certain social class or cultural group. As a consequence, members of different groups may have a different idea of the social behavior appropriate to a certain spatial structure, causing misunderstandings that produce social tensions. Recognizing functional patterns requires intensive study of the space and its use.

Spatial experience and emotional attachment

Physical and spatial sensations are both bodily and social experiences, making them fundamental to all human experience. All spatial experiences refer back to these fundamental experiences. Buildings are associated with people, and ensembles of buildings represent the relationships of people with each other. Associations are stored as experiences, and awaken positive or negative feelings.

Spatial structures are perceived in an emotional context, and spatial situations are associated with lifestyle. A place may be remembered, for instance, because of a particularly pleasant event, with an unimposing place remaining in the memory because a future life partner was seen there for the first time.

Individual and collective experiences

Many of these emotional links are based on individual experience, and therefore play no part in urban analysis. However, spatial situations can also stir emotions in society at large or in certain social groups. In some cases, a spatial situation can even produce opposite emotions in two different social groups, thereby creating conflicts.

Such places usually stand out from their surroundings. In general they are either particularly exposed places, like viewing platforms, or boundaries between two very different spatial structures, like riverbanks. Such locations are often spatially marked, creating a symbolic emphasis. In urban analysis, emotionally significant places must be recognized and documented. › Fig. 13

\\Example:
This system also applies to the ground plans of buildings, making the furnishings and locations of rooms with a specific purpose readable even to people using them for the first time. Rooms are full of codes that link to certain behaviors. Violating the rules by disregarding this code is socially prohibited.

\\Example:
Memorials relating to the two World Wars can produce very contradictory emotions in people, because they arouse both sorrow and guilt.

Fig.13:
Marking an emotionally significant place

Micro and macro levels

Cities are perceived on different levels. People usually have detailed knowledge of the area surrounding their home. In parallel with this, they incorporate the area into wider contexts without reference to detailed knowledge of these wider surroundings. This network is oriented on structural elements such as green corridors, the course of rivers or major traffic routes. Conspicuous places provide points of reference within it. Every location is therefore integrated into spatial structures on both the micro and the macro levels. Neither of these levels is autonomous. Instead, the two different levels overlap within any specific location.

IMPLEMENTATION

PREPARATION AND PLANNING PHASES

In theory, a surveyed area contains endless volumes of information, allowing a corresponding amount of analysis to be done. In practice, certain systems have become established within which analysis takes place. These systems can be divided up under the headings history, housing geography, and social structure. > Chapter Methods of analysis

Defining the subject matter

There are two reasons for conducting an urban analysis:

_ To reveal the overall picture: This means using urban analysis to obtain an overall picture of the area of investigation or of a whole urban area. Observed mistakes often trigger an urban analysis. These may include mass vacancy, poor building maintenance or major population fluctuations. The aim of the urban analysis is to replace suspicion with a definite diagnosis. In this case, several methods will be used on the area under investigation.

_ To provide an answer to a specific issue: This means analyzing specific features – for instance, the condition of existing residential buildings, the population's social situation, or the urban planning compatibility of a prospective building project. In this case, the evaluation must provide conclusions on the initial question.

Urban analyses are not formal or standardized procedures. This makes defining the subject matter before beginning an analysis indispensable. It is important to choose the right methods of analysis based on the reason for conducting the analysis. Failing to appropriately define the

\\ Note:
Housing geography describes both the spatial structure and the internal functions of the area under investigation. The most important elements are the functional structure, access structure, open space and green structure, and construction and development structure.

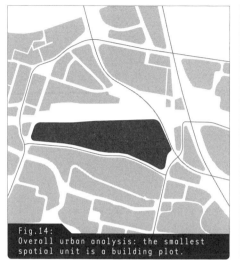

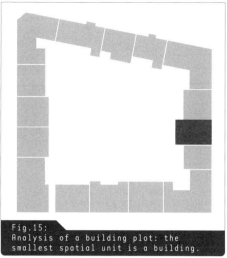

Fig.14:
Overall urban analysis: the smallest
spatial unit is a building plot.

Fig.15:
Analysis of a building plot: the
smallest spatial unit is a building.

subject matter can lead either to inadequate results or to collecting information that is of no use to the urban analysis. A rough impression of the situation within the area of analysis is therefore needed before the subject matter can be established.

Scale and spatial demarcation

Any information gained from an analysis is subject to scale. For instance, information relating to individual buildings may be relevant to a single building plot but useless for analyzing the whole city. It is not that small-scale analysis will always give an inaccurate picture of the area of investigation; it is simply that to provide useful results it must be seen in the wider city context. An overload of too much large-area information – a "data graveyard" – can distort findings on the area's relationship with the wider context. Compressing the data obtained into key points is an important part of urban analysis.

The smallest unit for a whole-city urban analysis is a building plot or neighborhood (scale 1:20,000 to 1:5000). This means that any analyzed characteristics must be seen in relation to this spatial area. Where the area under investigation is a single neighborhood, the smallest units are generally buildings and plots. Analyses involving a survey of only a few characteristics generally include a higher degree of detail. › Figs 14 and 15

Fig.16:
When analyzing the area of investigation, nearby areas must also be taken
into account.

Scale and degree of detail depend on how far the area under investigation extends; i.e. the larger the scale, the smaller the area of investigation. However, no planning area is autonomous. It will have many connections and reciprocal relationships with the surrounding areas, the city as a
whole, and even the wider region. Any urban analysis therefore has to look
beyond the area under investigation and take into account its integration
into the city's structure. › Figs 16–18

Continuation and monitoring

Continuing the analysis involves building on the investigation at particular intervals. Continuations may involve the same methods of analysis,
or expand on or modify them. This can lead to the analyzed facts experienc-
ing a change in emphasis.

\\ Note:
In this case, "building plot" describes a
housing development enclosed by roads or other
structural elements.

\\ Note:
An area of investigation's spatial integration
situation may have a positive impact – in the
case of nearby recreational facilities, for
instance – but it may also create conflicts, as
in the case of an industrial concern emitting
fumes near a residential area.

Fig.17:
Phenomena relevant to different areas
are active in any specific location: ...

Fig.18:
... residential building and street,
city and running water.

Monitoring in an urban analysis context means long-term observation of the area under investigation, usually by surveying a constant set
of values at regular intervals, comparing the results, and comparing with
other areas of investigation, or comparing several areas of investigation
with regard to certain values. Typical surveyed values include the number
of inhabitants and the demographic and social population characteristics.

Working with other specialist planners

It is often impossible for a single specialist planner to conduct an urban analysis, as many aspects require specialized knowledge. This means

> 🔖

🔖
\\ Note:
So that results can be compared, monitoring
demands clearly establish assessment factors
and working methods. It therefore generally
uses only standardized values. Comparability of
the surveyed areas should also be checked.

that, when preparing and setting an agenda for an urban analysis, the factors analyzed and the expertise needed must be clearly set out. In practice this involves setting up a working team or dividing the work between public planning authorities and specialist planners. Urban planners, architects and housing geographers usually supervise the main stages of an urban analysis, investigating land use, transport, housing and construction structures. Specialized analysis may require, for instance, transport system planners or historians. Open space and ecological issues are generally handled by open space planners or landscape architects. Biologists, meteorologists and geographers make specialized contributions on the open space and ecological situation. If analyzing the social structure necessitates extensive surveys or statistical work, social scientists will have to be included. Participation initiatives will require moderators.

OBTAINING AND PROCESSING DATA

Urban analysis involves obtaining extensive amounts of data. Permission to access these materials must be agreed or arranged as early as the availability and capability of the relevant authority will permit.

Urban analysis involves collecting and processing very different form of data:

_ Data in paper form, such as printed reports and plans
_ Digital data, such as planning documents, text and image files
_ Information gained from personally visiting the site › Chapter Working in the area under analysis
_ Information from conversations with third parties › Chapter Working in the area under analysis

› Chapter Working in the area under analysis

\\ Tip:
When establishing a working group, areas of research should be clearly demarcated to avoid redundancy. If necessary, the chronological sequence of the analysis should be firmly established, as the results produced by one specialist planner may have implications for another's evaluation.

\\ Tip:
Before beginning an urban analysis, it should be established whether there will be any charge for providing or preparing necessary data materials, and who should be liable for this.

If an urban analysis is to be published, someone must check the copyright status of the materials used, which should be identified in the publication. Data protection laws apply to the publication of personal data. The data protection authorities responsible should be contacted so that rules for dealing with these materials can be agreed.

Historical information

Historical maps, publications on the city's past and chronicles are important reference works for a historical analysis. It is generally a good idea to talk to city archives and libraries. In smaller cities, these services are often provided by honorary appointees. They will however only provide a collection of historical materials such as photos and local publications, rather than scientifically prepared information. The evaluation of such historical raw materials is very labor-intensive, and is usually only required in the case of a scientific investigation.

Maps as a basis

Scale maps are an essential practical tool in any urban analysis. Maps may provide information or be a medium for contextualizing the different results of analysis. There are no national or international standards for maps as a basis for urban analysis, meaning that the availability and technical quality of the materials have to be checked at the beginning of the analysis. Because they may use different projections, not all sets of maps are compatible. This means that they cannot always be used within the same document. Maps for urban analysis use are usually produced and distributed by state bodies.

Topographical map

A topographical map shows geographical features and spatial objects on the earth's surface. The contour lines in particular make this kind of map useful for an urban analysis. Scales of between 1:5000 and 1:50,000 are used for urban analysis purposes. Maps are generally available as

Fig.19:
Topographical map

Fig.20:
Real estate map

› Fig. 19

digital data grids. To some extent, groups of objects or geographic features can be provided as layers, each printed with one set of data. › Fig. 19

Real estate map

The real estate map is used as a basis for the geodata, enabling numerous connections with other specialist data. The real estate map is the visual part of the land register, showing the ownership of all parcels of land.

The real estate map shows spatial and topographical features as well as plots of land. Its inclusion of extensive information on objects and land plots makes the real estate map particularly interesting to urban analysts. Real estate maps note particular attributes of plots and objects, e.g. land use or number of stories in buildings. Identical or similar objects are organized using the precise definitions in an object catalogue. These are arranged into separate layers, sorting the map's content by subject. The real estate map is also part of the land register map information system – i.e. the database contains extensive data on the area in addition to the real estate map's visual information. › Fig. 20

Real estate maps are kept digitally by land registry offices and can be edited by others if converted into vector files. Before referring to the real estate map, it should be ascertained what object and plot-related information it can provide. Conversely, it may be necessary to narrow down a large amount of available data.

The usual file formats for transfer into a CAD (Computer Aided Design) system are *.DXF (Drawing Interchange Format) or *.DWG (Drawing, a file format from the Autodesk product range). If files from the land registry information system are to be transferred, other data formats must be used.

Aerial photographs are available taken vertically or at an angle. Non-distorted true to scale vertical images – called orthophotos – are often used, as these are comparable to other map materials and can therefore be used in combination with them. Together with real estate maps, aerial photographs can provide important information on object coordinates. In particular, this helps to pinpoint green infrastructure. Aerial photographs are also an effective way of illustrating analysis results because they can be easily understood by lay people. › Fig. 21

Depending on the area of investigation, an urban analysis may require large-scale detailed maps. For instance, utility companies will be able to provide maps showing underground supply lines.

Geoinformation systems (GIS systems) are used to manage and visualize spatial data. Many evaluations can be made based on them. With GIS systems, the emphasis is generally on storing extensive bodies of digital data in the form of databanks and making connections between them through evaluation rather than expressing information in maps. The reference values for these connections are spatial features, which are recorded graphically in geometric form – as with a CAD system. These drawings are usually based on standard maps such as the topographical map.

Conducting an urban analysis using a GIS system requires extensive prior research. The availability of compatible sets of data is very important. Data transfers from other systems can lead to data being lost during formatting, necessitating time-consuming manual inputting of data. The

\\ Note:
If the real estate map covers a large area, it may be a good idea to exchange test data (extracts) before submitting a final set of data.

\\ Note:
Real estate maps are technical maps with limited relevance to lay people. They must be extensively revised graphically before they can be used to illustrate analysis results.

Fig.21:
Vertical aerial photograph (ortho-
photo)

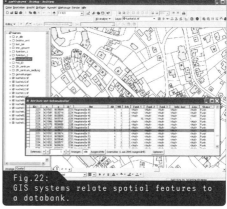

Fig.22:
GIS systems relate spatial features to
a databank.

commonest providers of data records are public bodies, but private concerns are increasingly providing spatial data records. One's own survey results can be incorporated into the GIS system as well as external data records. › Fig. 22

Field computers   Field computers allow standardized survey results to be collated digitally onsite. The results being entered can be assigned to the correct location by clicking on a touchscreen showing a map or by matching with coordinates calculated by an integrated GPS (Global Positioning System) receiver. A GIS system evaluates the submitted data. › Fig. 23

Existing plans and analyses

Areas under investigation have often been previously subjected to planning and analysis. These materials must be evaluated in the light of certain restrictions, and of other information. Formal planning works set out regulations on, for instance, the type and extent of land use for

\\ Note:
The use of GIS systems for long-term area
observation (monitoring) is particularly
interesting, as the inclusion of the most
up-to-date sets of data makes it relatively
easy to create new evaluations and evaluative
maps.

Fig.23:
An example of a field computer

construction, the situation of any feature for which the immediate surroundings must be kept clear, or the extent of flood-risk areas. Sometimes specialist assessments are available, analyzing particularly important factors in the area of investigation and its surroundings. These include:

_ Ecological specialist articles containing information on existing valuable green infrastructure › Chapter Analysis of open space and green structure
_ Sound protection reports dealing with noise pollution – existing or anticipated in connection with planned projects
_ Transport reports analyzing existing traffic pressures and the capacity of existing transport facilities, networks and systems › Chapter Analysis of transport structure
_ Retail reports analyzing the retail structures of the survey area › Chapter Analysis of land use structure

Any relevant information from the available reports will be incorporated into the urban analysis. Its interactions with other factors and its implications for future urban planning will be investigated. Depending on its importance, this information will be represented in a scale map.

› 🗋

Data and
statistics on
residents

In general, administrative authorities are required to carry out regular analyses of the population structure. This involves analyzing the whole population of districts or statistical survey areas under certain headings. The area of investigation for an urban analysis is generally not identical with any of these statistical survey areas, making the possibilities for applying the data to a specific investigation area limited. To make an

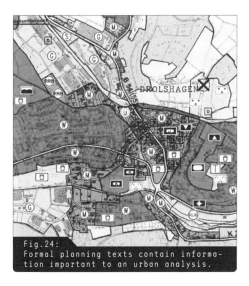

Fig.24:
Formal planning texts contain information important to an urban analysis.

evaluation relevant to the area of investigation, a new census area has to be marked out.

This demarcation must be done by administrative departments, because external experts do not have access to data on residents. In order to satisfy data protection requirements, data sufficient for building up a small-area picture can be provided only after extensive agreements have been reached between urban analysts and the authorities responsible.

When analyzing the population structure, it is particularly useful to supplement surveys restricted to specific reference dates with studies of developments over time, and compare them with other survey areas, making it essential to have access to suitable comparative data.

\\ Note:
In practice, all existing plans and analyses are requested from the relevant authorities in the early stages of an urban analysis. Many planning texts can be downloaded from the Internet (see Fig. 24).

\\ Note:
The term "census area" describes a continuous area for which particular characteristics such as the average age of residents or the number of homes can be assigned.

WORKING IN THE AREA UNDER ANALYSIS
Taking an inventory in the field

Field work in the area of investigation is an essential part of urban analysis. Most analysis results can only be obtained by recording the existing situation on-site. Spatial qualities and atmospheric impressions only become apparent to an urban analyst visiting the area of investigation. It may be necessary to view the area at different times of day, or on different days of the week.

You will need to have suitable documents prepared for textually and graphically recording the information gained from the site visit. The volume of information recorded and the nature of the spaces involved will vary depending on the dimensions and degree of detail of the analysis. The documents must be appropriate to the volume of information and the spatial relationships involved. Unsuitable documents with excessive notes can turn the subsequent evaluation into a labor-intensive piece of detective work. › Fig. 25

Parties to the onsite visit will generally evaluate their own notes. More extensive surveys, however, involve assembling an editing team. In this case, a standard way of listing analysis results must be agreed upon to preclude subsequent misunderstandings. Standardized questionnaires are particularly suited to this.

Topographic or real estate maps are used to record the onsite visit. Different scales are used depending on the dimensions and degree of detail of the analysis:

_ For analyzing the urban integration situation, topographical maps or aerial photographs with a scale of between 1:5000 and 1:20,000 are suitable.

\\ Tip:
To prevent any information gaps in the subsequent evaluation, the site visit must be preceded by thorough preparation. Such an error may result in time-consuming extra research, particularly if long traveling distances are involved.

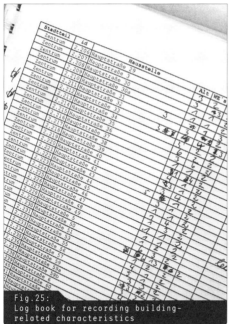

Fig.25:
Log book for recording building-
related characteristics

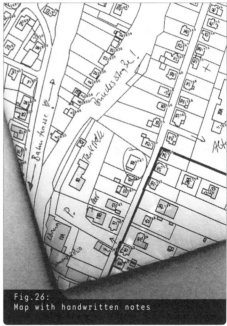

Fig.26:
Map with handwritten notes

_ For recording housing geography features, real estate maps with a scale of 1:1000 are generally used. When preparing these maps, any layers that are not relevant to the site visit should be left out.

_ For recording plot or building level data, real estate maps with a scale of 1:500 are used. Larger-scale maps tend to result in paper formats that are too large to handle easily in the field. It may be a good idea to combine the map and the survey sheet, with the map allowing individual objects to be pinpointed and the survey sheet allowing analysis results to be listed. The survey sheet will be created as a standardized questionnaire, to prevent any survey criteria from being overlooked during the inventory. › Fig. 26

Cameras are generally used to document the area of investigation. It is often a good idea to note the places where photos were taken on a map, to allow the photographs to be put in a spatial context during subsequent analysis.

Citizen participation, contact with local operators

Residents have extensive detailed knowledge of their own neighborhood. Others active in the area, such as business people and those who run local initiatives, will also have knowledge of local conditions and how they affect people. These sources of information should be included in any analysis.

Regulated contact with residents can be achieved using a series of methods. This is useful for assessing the impact on people within the area of investigation of all the factors and conflicts involved, rather than for gaining detailed information on the locality.

Residents'
meeting

A residents' meeting is a frequently used method of citizen participation, usually with little preparation. In practice, residents' meetings where no specific action is discussed have a low perceived level of impact on the residents and are therefore not well attended. Organizing a residents' meeting is therefore only recommended where both specific measures and general plans of action are to be discussed. It is also a good idea to present residents with the first urban analysis evaluations, to provide an object and structure for the subsequent discussion. As some residents will avoid the public exposure of meetings, this method will not produce a representative sample of residents. The meeting place chosen should always have a low associated inhibition level – i.e. should be within the investigated area.

Individual
public
consultation

Preparing, carrying out and evaluating an individual public consultation is very time-consuming, and they are therefore only included in urban analyses that require an extensive social structure analysis. Individual consultations and their evaluation require the assistance of social scientists.

Individual consultations may take the form of narrative interviews or standardized questionnaires. Standardized processes make it easier

\\ Tip:
A visit to the site will generally result
in spontaneous contacts with residents. Such
meetings should not be avoided – careful
inquiries may provide useful information.

to evaluate the results. Mass-mailed questionnaires generally have a low response rate. They do not provide a representative cross section of the population structure either.

Conducting several specialist consultations allows a large body of location-specific specialist knowledge to be gathered in a relatively short time. Specialist consultations are discussion groups focusing on specific subjects, with specialists in the relevant field invited to attend. Participants generally include specialist representatives from the relevant authorities plus those active in the area under discussion. These may be people working for welfare organizations, voluntary workers or representatives of local entrepreneurship.

METHODS OF ANALYSIS

Urban analysis of a particular area may include investigations of one or more issues, e.g. different land uses and transport organization in the area of investigation. As already stated, these sectoral analyses are simply abstract, partial representations of the reality. In practice, however, they simplify the analysis process, as the complex interplay of all values cannot be recorded or presented. At the same time, any urban analysis should note as many interactions between these sectoral analyses as possible. Put simply, urban analyses begin by dismantling the area under investigation like a motor, and then use the knowledge of the individual parts thus gained plus their interactions to put it back together again.

Urban analysis is not formally regulated, and so there are unlimited ways of carrying it out. For this reason, only the sectoral analysis types most commonly used in practical town planning are included here.

HISTORICAL ANALYSIS

Historical analysis inquires into the causative events for the creation and composition of the analyzed area, or significant influences on it. Events in recent history may therefore also be significant. Historical analysis is not limited to identifying the stylistic roots of existing urban structures. It records and interprets events that had implications for the spatial development or the area of investigation. › Figs 27 and 28

There are two possible fields of reference for a historical analysis:

_ The area of investigation as a whole: This involves evaluating which historical events and circumstances have influenced the overall structure of the area of investigation.
_ The area of investigation as the sum of its parts: This involves researching individual structural features to determine whether they are or were typical of particular developments.

Historical events include spatial measures such as the building of town fortifications or reconstruction after a fire. Many historical events, however, have implications for the area of investigation's spatial development without themselves being specific spatial measures. For instance, economic circumstances such as a boom or decline in the regional economy may have affected the area of investigation's spatial development.

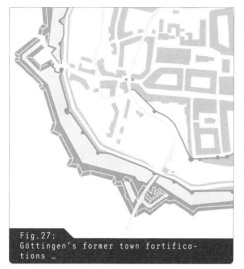

Fig.27:
Göttingen's former town fortifications …

Fig.28:
… are now part of a vital recreational
area.

Recording
individual
features

Whether the area of investigation will be analyzed as a whole or on the level of separate plots is generally decided by the number of historically significant buildings. In a plot-by-plot analysis, buildings are assessed individually, and any historically relevant features documented. Buildings are usually assessed according to a standardized catalog of criteria, then – if possible – assigned to various building types. Commonly used criteria include the building's age, and the extent and state of preservation of any historical stylistic features. The next step is to mark these buildings on a map based on their features. This helps to ascertain the spatial distribution of different building types in real space and the number of groups of significant buildings. > Figs 29 and 30

Interactions
in the area of
investigation

In some rare cases, the spatial characteristics of an area of investigation can be explained by a historical event. This would be the case, for instance, for a comprehensively planned neighborhood built within a limited period of time. More usually, however, an area of investigation's spatial characteristics have been influenced by several different events and circumstances. These events will generally have occurred at different times, leading to repeated remolding of the area of investigation, and leaving traces on various places within the area of investigation (buildings from different eras). Different events may have molded a single place, with one set of circumstances overlying another (e.g. 1950s buildings within the ground plan of a medieval town). The density and distribution of analyzed features will show whether the area of investigation's development

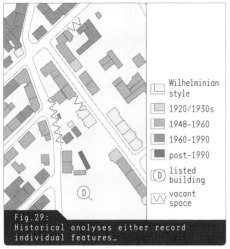

Wilhelminian style

1920/1930s

1948-1960

1960-1990

post-1990

listed building

vacant space

Fig.29:
Historical analyses either record
individual features…

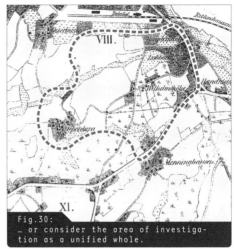

Fig.30:
… or consider the area of investigation as a unified whole.

> 📎

can be traced back to a small number of historical developments and circumstances, or whether a very diverse historical development pattern lies
behind its present characteristics.

Context beyond
the area of
investigation

Historical analysis involves working out the relationship of the area
of investigation to surrounding areas or to the city as a whole, to understand its context within the development of the city. It must also be ascertained whether the area of investigation is typical of the overall development of the city, or whether it has played a special role in history.

Conclusion

Thorough historical research is particularly important in areas significant to the city's planning history. However, areas initially considered
to have no historical significance may reveal typical development processes
in the course of a historical analysis, demonstrating aspects of the area of

\\ Note:
When examining the area of investigation as
a whole, historical maps are generally used
to analyze historical development. Due to
differences in scale and reproduction, these
cannot usually be compared with modern-day
maps.

\\ Note:
Land use intensity often correlates with construction density, meaning that the results of
the building and settlement analysis should be
compared with the results of the use structure
analysis.

investigation's identity and ongoing development. When interpreting historical analyses, it is important to keep to describing the facts that have clearly influenced the area of investigation's development. Discursions on general city history, e.g. succession, documentary references or town twinning arrangements, can be excluded from an urban analysis, as they generally have no influence on the properties of an area of investigation.

ANALYSIS OF LAND USE STRUCTURE

Analysis of land use structure involves investigating the real uses that exist or predominate within the area of investigation and the interrelations of different uses.

Land use
intensity

Land use intensity can be described using statistical values. A ratio is created from all the area of investigation's compiled characteristics. One application of this is to calculate the proportion of surface area under different land uses by expressing the proportion of the overall surface area taken up by each individual use. However, features may also be documented in this way – the number of workplaces, for instance. Land use intensity can also be described as a density value. This involves calculating the relationship of certain features to units of surface area. One frequently used density value is population density relative to settled area.

Recording
individual
features

Analysis of land use structure involves determining real use relative to spatial units. A spatial unit in this context may be an open space or a building. If the facts are being recorded by area, and the area is occupied by a building, the building's function is the determining factor for its use type. For instance, if the building on the site contains apartments, then the designation will be "residential" regardless of any open space near the plot.

Analyses of whole cities or investigation areas of comparable size establish land uses for whole building plots (or neighborhoods), i.e. areas containing several plots. As these spatial units often have no homogenous land use structure, they determine the predominating use instead. District land use structure analyses are generally done plot by plot, i.e. determining the land use of every plot, or the number of plots in a particular land use area. This involves recording the surface area used for traffic and green spaces as well as built-up plots.

Analyses of land use structure may be restricted to recording building use, leaving open space use to the analysis of open space and green structure. This division of labor is particularly suitable when land use is

Residential
Mixed use
Commercial
Secondary facilities

Fig.31:
Depending on scale and the degree of detail required, a land use structure analysis may be performed plot by plot …

Residential
Mixed use
Commercial

Fig.32:
… or with reference to particular building plots.

being recorded story by story. Such highly detailed analyses are usually only applied to small areas of investigation. › Figs 31 and 32

Land use is generally researched by visiting the site, i.e. visually. However, much information can be gained from real estate map data. In some cases, authorities may provide data on surface area use from their GIS systems. › Chapter Obtaining and processing data Another useful source of information is the directory of firms kept by some business associations. There is however a risk that the postal address of a business is within the area of investigation, but not its production sites.

The land uses present within an area of investigation can be differentiated to varying degrees depending on the degree of detail needed. Subsequent division of the results into headings and subheadings is recommended. › Fig. 33

Residential

Generalized residential functions can be differentiated by the building structures, e.g. detached, semi-detached and row housing, or multi-story apartments with open or closed building forms. Special residence types – such as sheltered housing and homes – are shown separately, as they make particular requirements of local suppliers and transport connections.

Residential buildings
as part of a row

Multi-story
apartment buildings
(open building form)

Multi-story
apartment buildings
(closed building form)

Individual houses

Mixed construction
areas

Commercial
construction areas

Urban wasteland

Residential and
access roads

Other routes/roads

Parking areas

O Retail of
everyday goods

Fig.33:
Land use structure analysis map with key

Commercial

Commercial land uses are differentiated according to the degree of disruption they cause – i.e. their compatibility with residential land use:

- _ Industrial trade creates the greatest degree of disruption, and is therefore confined to planning-regulated industrial districts.
- _ Trade encompasses all commercial land uses. These exist mainly in planning-regulated industrial districts. They include manufacturing, haulage and storage, wholesale, city depots and craft enterprises.
- _ Non-disruptive trade includes types of business compatible with residential land use. Most of these are in the service or retail sectors.

43

The output of the service sector is non-material, and depends on direct contact between people. Service sector trade can therefore be differentiated according to the degree of dealings with the public:

- _ Customer-oriented service sector trade describes facilities that regularly deal with the public, such as travel agents or leisure services
- _ Non-customer-oriented service sector trade includes offices

Service sector operations may also be suppliers, meaning that supply and non-supply service sector operations can be differentiated. Service sector operations with a supply function include doctor's surgeries and offices of postal and parcel services.

Retail describes businesses that sell products to the end user. By contrast, wholesale dealers sell to sellers.

In a district-level analysis, retail facilities for everyday essentials are additionally identified because they are important local amenities for residents. Local providers of everyday essentials should not be farther away (as the crow flies) than a 500 m radius (for a good local amenity situation) or 700 m (for a satisfactory local amenity situation) from any place of residence. Everyday essentials include groceries and everyday luxury items, drinks and health care and grooming products. Services such as doctors' surgeries and post offices may be included in the evaluation of the local amenity situation.

Mixed land use describes a combination of residential and other – usually residence-compatible – land uses. Different combinations – for instance, residential and restaurants, residential and offices – can be differentiated, depending on the degree of detail of the urban analysis.

🗋
\\ Note:
Retail can be subdivided according to many
different criteria, for instance the marketing
type (self-service, supermarket, specialist
shop, specialist market etc.), centrality, area
served, branch group, and shopping area.

Identifying different degrees of combination to show whether residence or commerce is the dominant land use is also common.

Public amenities
Public amenities are public facilities open to all – particularly kindergartens and daycare facilities, churches, cultural facilities and authorities. Open-air facilities such as play areas and cemeteries may also be recorded as public amenities.

Leisure and social facilities may be public amenities, but may also be run by commercial concerns. Depending on their nature – public or private – they may be evaluated as public amenities or customer-oriented service-sector commerce.

Hotel and catering
Catering includes all facilities offering catering services, e.g. restaurants, snack bars, cafes, liquor stores and ice-cream parlors. Hotels include guesthouses with service.

Entertainment venues
Facilities intended for entertainment and relaxation, such as discos and amusement arcades, are entertainment venues. As they generally create a fairly high level of disruption, they are treated as a separate category in urban analysis.

Plant
Plant includes facilities or buildings used to regulate and maintain various types of supply for the urban area or to control particular commercial processes. These include gas regulator stations, transformer stations, and sewage plants. Many of these facilities are surrounded by protection zones, i.e. a certain distance must be maintained between the plant and surrounding land uses.

Transport
Transport structure analysis differentiates between different types of road or different financial responsibilities for roads. In either case, land use structure analysis can also provide findings on transport facilities.

Transport-related constructions, such as rail stations and bus terminals, may be recorded as such, or listed as public amenities.

Open-space uses
Important open-space uses, generally included in analysis of open space and green structure, can be incorporated into the analysis of land use structure instead. They include parks and play areas, which can be classified as public amenities.

Vacancy
Vacancy is a functional deficiency. Mass vacancy generally indicates that an area is unattractive, usually due to urban planning disruptions or

> 📎

mistakes. It is difficult to establish and prove vacancy, partly because it is not always obvious to the eye and partly because it takes long-term observation to know how long buildings have been vacant.

Vacancy in residential and commercial buildings are differentiated, as these often have different causes and require different measures. It is also wise to differentiate between part of a building and a whole building standing vacant. > Fig. 34

Other land uses

Unusual uses that occur only once or rarely within the area of investigation are generally identified and labeled individually in the evaluation plan, to avoid lengthy and confusing keys on maps.

Garages, shelters and similar facilities can be recorded as secondary facilities.

Granulation

The main task of land use analysis is to investigate subdivisions with comparable land use types and thereby determine granulation. Recording these main areas is particularly important for identifying any disruptions between different land use areas. Land uses each produce their own level of disruption, but also an entitlement to protection. High land use gradients – neighborhoods with very different protection requirements and degrees of disruption – generally lead to conflicts, while shallower use gradients – neighborhoods with similar protection requirements and degrees of disruption – have low conflict potentials.

Context beyond
the area of
investigation

When investigating subdivisions with comparable land use types, the areas adjoining the area of investigation must also be considered, as these can also be the cause of disruptions or protection requirements.

📎

\\ Note:
Aside from judging by appearances, vacancy can
be deduced from buildings' electricity use.
This method involves the energy supply companies, and is therefore rarely practical.

Fig.34:
Vacancy may indicate that a structure
is not fit for purpose.

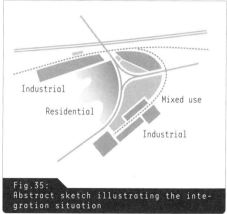

Industrial

Residential

Mixed use

Industrial

Fig.35:
Abstract sketch illustrating the integration situation

An area's granulation reflects land use distribution and the area of investigation's land use balance. This relationship also expresses the purpose and centrality of the area of investigation in the broader urban context. Categories are generally based on the different planning area types, e.g. › Fig. 35

_ Purely residential area
_ Residential area with a limited number of residence-compatible workplaces
_ Mixed area
_ Inner city and city center
_ Commercial area
_ Industrial area
_ Special area

Conclusion   During the final evaluation, the purpose of the area of investigation must be taken into account, to determine which findings harmonize with that purpose, and which contradict it. › Chapter Interpretation and illustration A central task of land use structure analysis is to reveal any land use conflicts. A distinction must be made between the cause, e.g. incompatible combinations, and the effect, e.g. increased vacancies. › Fig. 36

Fig.36:
Mixed land use structure: appropriate
to area of investigation or source of
land use conflicts?

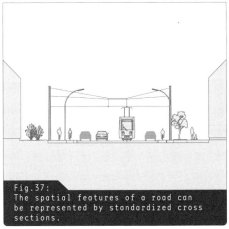

Fig.37:
The spatial features of a road can
be represented by standardized cross
sections.

ANALYSIS OF TRANSPORT STRUCTURE

Transport structure analysis investigates existing transport facilities in the area under investigation and the connection and integration of the area of investigation into transport networks. In this context, roads are public spaces as well as transport constructions, making them critical to perception of the area of investigation. Road design should therefore also be the object of urban analysis. Often characteristic features can be identified for each road. It makes sense to record the standard of improvements to each part of the road network. These represent both the capacity and user-friendliness of the various areas of road, e.g. › Fig. 37

_ Proportion of road width to adjacent buildings
_ Division of road space into driving lanes and side areas
_ Type, shape and size of road spaces
_ Road furniture and surface materials
_ Lighting apparatus and lighting types

A highly detailed analysis of transport structure will require a specialist engineer. Transport reports suitable for urban analysis purposes may already be available. As well as analyzing types of transport (passenger or freight), purpose of transport (shopping, professional or leisure journeys etc.), and distances (source traffic, destination traffic, internal and transit traffic), these are likely to contain data on traffic pressures.

› []

Transport can be analyzed according to many different structural features. In urban analysis, it is mainly differentiated according to the type of transportation used, i.e. motorized traffic, local public transport and foot and cycle traffic.

Motorized traffic

Moving traffic

The first step in analyzing moving traffic is to rank the roads in the area of investigation according to their capacity, e.g. › Fig. 38

  _ Expressway / trunk road
  _ Main traffic route
  _ Connecting road
  _ Main collector road
  _ District access road
  _ Other road significant for transport
  _ Agricultural and forestry routes

This kind of analysis determines the area of investigation's road transport network structure. In most cases, all its roads form a hierarchical network; i.e. the traffic in the network is unevenly distributed. Road types are based on a kind of division of labor. Heavily used roads concentrate the traffic, while moderate to low-use roads distribute it. Parts of the network can be assigned functions based on their traffic pressure: connection (heavy load), access (moderate load), and stopping (low pressure).

› ◗

Deviations from this schema tend to lead to conflicts.

Dormant traffic

Parked vehicles (and non-functional vehicles) are described as dormant traffic. An urban analysis generally notes the provision and uptake density of public parking spaces. Public parking spaces may be found on

Main traffic route

Connecting road

Main collector road

District access road

Fig.38:
Road transport network analysis map

public roads or in designated collection facilities (ground-level car parks, underground garages, or multi-story car parks). These are managed in different ways, ranging from non-paying parking space, to timed parking, to a charge for parking. › Fig. 39

Different land uses in an area of investigation cause different parking space requirements. This means that the spatial location of parking spaces in relation to different land uses is of interest as well as parking space provision.

Context beyond the area of investigation

Transport structure analysis involves the area of investigation's internal access network as well as how the area of investigation is integrated into the road traffic network of the city or region as a whole. This means determining the shape of any transport network within which the area of investigation is contained – a radial or ring system, for instance. An area of investigation generally has traffic networks that cover different units of distance overlapping within it. Long-range transport systems are a direct

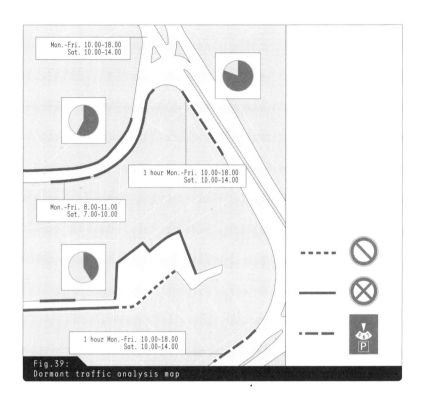

Mon.-Fri. 10.00-18.00
Sat. 10.00-14.00

1 hour Mon.-Fri. 10.00-18.00
Sat. 10.00-14.00

Mon.-Fri. 8.00-11.00
Sat. 7.00-10.00

1 hour Mon.-Fri. 10.00-18.00
Sat. 10.00-14.00

Fig.39:
Dormant traffic analysis map

means of transport to beyond the area of investigation, but also burden it with traffic headed elsewhere, with the associated fumes and noise emissions. Depending on where these networks and functions come together spatially, they may lead to disruptions within the area of investigation.
> Fig. 40

\\ Note:
Uptake intensity is investigated within a representative time period. This involves calculating the number of occupied parking spaces in relation to the total number. An occupancy rate graph showing the degree of use over the course of a day or week can also be compiled.

Main traffic route

Connecting road

Rail route

Fig.40:
Traffic integration analysis map

Local public transport

Local public transport describes short-distance passenger services accessible to all. These generally follow routes and schedules. Analysis of local public transport investigates the availability of and service at stops, and the network's structure. A distinction is made between different local public transport systems:

_ Railbound systems (regional trains, suburban trains, city railways, subways, trams)
_ Scheduled bus system
_ Other systems (e.g. on-call shared taxi, citizens' bus)

The provision of stops is an important factor. A maximum distance of 300 m from the relevant residential and working areas (as the crow flies) represents good network access, while a maximum of 500 m represents

satisfactory network access. This analysis should take into account topographical conditions, existing pedestrian facilities (e.g. pedestrian crossings) as well as spatial barriers that require a detour. The level of improvements (e.g. lifts serving rail platforms, high curbs in relation to low floor technology) also affects accessibility.

The quality of local public transport depends significantly on frequent service at stops, as well as the network speed. Punctuality, regular scheduled connections, long running hours and mechanisms for speeding up public transport (e.g. bus lanes and automated priority for local public transport at traffic lights) are important measures of quality when analyzing local public transport. > Fig. 41

Context beyond the area of investigation

The area of investigation may be contained within a centrally oriented or decentralized network. Centralized networks have a single node

53

where passengers can change for other route lines or transport systems. Decentralized networks have several nodes. Many networks fall somewhere between these two systems. The upshot of all this is that when assessing local public transport the area of investigation's spatial proximity to these nodes is as important as the number of stops it contains.

Foot and cycle traffic
Depending on the degree of provision in the area of investigation, pedestrian and cycling facilities may be independent elements or simply parts of the network.

Analyses of the footpath system only include independently managed footpaths, with walking routes along the sides of roads only included in very detailed transport structure analyses.

An analysis of cycle traffic will generally record all cycling facilities, and distinguish between cycle paths along the side of roads, cycling zones (marked routes within general traffic lanes), independent cycle paths, and cycle roads etc.

The improvement standard of the pedestrian and cycle network and its safety systems are the major factors determining connection quality between different parts of the area of investigation and its surroundings. For this reason, the nodes of all facilities for conducting cycle traffic should be recorded, not just the safe crossings (e.g. crossings at intersections and other ground-level crossings). Areas that are particularly inconvenient or dangerous should also be named. All land uses within the area of investigation that represent points of origin or destinations for various forms of transport should also be recorded. › Fig. 42

Context beyond the area of investigation

Footpaths and cycle paths connecting the area of investigation with its surroundings or with neighboring districts are of particular interest to urban analysis. For analyses of whole cities, or of areas of investigation of comparable size, it is a good idea to divide the pedestrian and cycle routes into leisure and everyday networks. While leisure networks generally represent access to regional recreation facilities, everyday networks are based on reaching the foci of urban activity as quickly as possible.

Concluding observations on transport structure analysis
Different land uses have different access needs – i.e. they require transport systems and facilities of different dimensions. The task is to

Controlled crossing

Footpath

Sensitive use

(H) Public transport stop

Fig.42:
Foot traffic analysis map

identify the varying degrees of provision and any disruptions, along with the cost and quality of access provision. Conversely, all the land uses in an area of investigation have varying rights to protection from dust and noise emissions. High pressures from motorized traffic tend to impact on the quality of nearby housing and the quality of time spent in an urban space. They also act as spatial barriers, dividing the area of investigation. At the same time, high traffic pressures on roads can represent centers of urban life. A concluding evaluation should weigh up all these significant factors.

The different kinds of transport also make competing demands on urban space. One transport network's high standard of development may be detrimental to the functioning of another. For instance, plentiful bus lanes may be convenient for users of local public transport, but impact on the capacity for individual motor transport.

Fig.43:
Roads must be evaluated in the light
of many different interacting factors.

All networks should be assessed for whether they support spatial orientation by being readily comprehensible and easy to remember. Good orientation increases network users' comfort and sense of security. › Fig. 43

ANALYSIS OF OPEN SPACE AND GREEN STRUCTURE

Analysis of open space and green structure analysis has two main tasks:

1. To represent open-space infrastructure elements and their right to protection under species protection and ecology law. Urban analysts do not generally perform their own ecological analyses, instead taking any information relevant to the area of analysis' spatial development from external specialist reports.
2. To investigate the use and aesthetic quality of open space and the interactions between open space and the housing structure. The spatial qualities of the green and open space structure are personally surveyed and evaluated by urban analysts.

Space-related features

Like a land use structure analysis, open space and green structure analysis records all real use of open spaces. Unlike land use structure analysis, the object of the process is the use of the open spaces on the plots involved. The type of open space represented by each individual space is recorded. As the subject matter overlaps with land use structure, this labor-intensive process is often left out of urban analysis, in which case

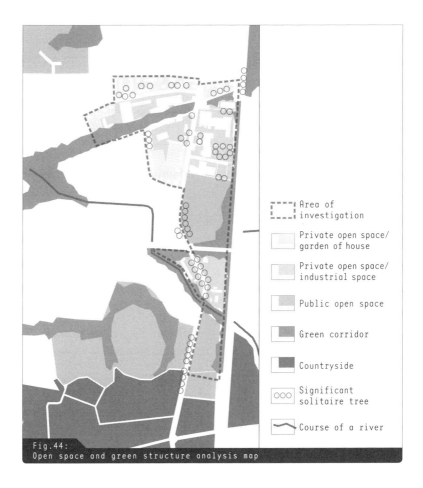

Fig. 44:
Open space and green structure analysis map

Legend:

- Area of investigation
- Private open space/ garden of house
- Private open space/ industrial space
- Public open space
- Green corridor
- Countryside
- Significant solitaire tree
- Course of a river

the main features of analyzing open space and green structure are simply differentiated. These spaces are differentiated primarily by their owner-ship, recording › Fig. 44

- _ Public open spaces, e.g. public parks, fairgrounds, waterside prom-enades, bodies of water
- _ Public open spaces associated with certain facilities, e.g. school and kindergarten playgrounds, zoos
- _ Semi-public open spaces, e.g. the inner courtyard of an apartment complex, an office building's open spaces
- _ Private open spaces, e.g. gardens, company grounds

Landscapes are generally only differentiated by open space type in the case of a whole-city analysis. The following are recorded:

_ Cultivated space (e.g. farmland, pasture, vineyards)
_ Woods (e.g. protected woodland, recreational woodland)
_ Other spaces (e.g. moorland, marsh, bodies of water)

Structural
elements
with a spatial
presence

As well as recording open spaces, open space and green structure analysis also records natural structuring features that have a particular effect on the space around them. These structural features include:

_ Notable solitaire trees and groups of trees
_ Linear structures such as avenues of trees or hedges
_ Green corridors

Spatial features of the green and open space structure are hard to designate on a map using a standardized key, as so many of them are highly individual. When documenting analysis results, it is therefore a good idea to use spatial sketch plans or abstract icons. › Fig. 45

Evaluating
features

The first step in analyzing open and green structure is to evaluate the intrinsic value of individual features. Elements that have particular significance in one or more of the following four categories are evaluated:

_ Historical significance: significant garden architecture or cultural history elements (e.g. historical parks and elements of the cultural landscape)
_ Spatial experience: spatial qualities, such as the interplay of planting and open space or the cumulative effect of open space and topography
_ Recreational value: areas with special recreational functions (e.g. parks and municipal woods near housing areas)
_ Functional value: uses of open space and green structure are important as part of surface area-related land use recording
_ Protection value: elements of the open space and green structure protected by law

Protection
zones and
protected
elements

An inventory of all protection zones and protected elements taken from the relevant planning documents and specialist reports must be incorporated into the urban analysis:

_ Protected zones where particular land uses are prohibited: Protection of animal and plant life, landscape characteristics (e.g.

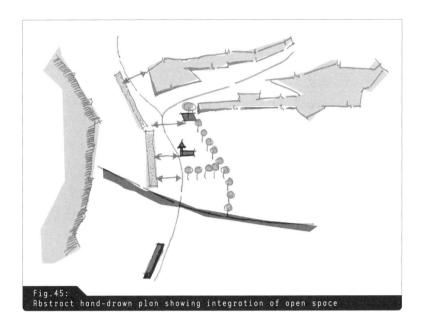

conservation areas and protected landscapes), and protection of drinking water resources and fresh air corridors

_ Protected infrastructure elements: Protection of individual elements for animal and plant life, such as solitaire trees, hedges or banks

For an urban analysis, all protected zones and protected elements relevant to the area of investigation's urban development are pinpointed on a scale map. › Fig. 46

\\ Note:
The recreational value of open spaces varies according to land use intensity. Open spaces close to settlements often have many visitors, whereas continuous countryside has proportionally fewer visitors.

Fig.46:
Protection zone analysis map

Interactions in
the area under
investigation
The interaction of open space and housing structure is the most interesting part of open space analysis. The proportional surface area and the spatial distribution of each type of open space can be determined from an inventory of open spaces. Calculating this enables us to determine the degree of provision of specific recreational spaces for the area under investigation. This is generally according to the population of the area of investigation.

Residential estates with many small units on the edge of cities generally have houses with gardens, reducing the need for public open spaces. Closed, heavily built-up inner-city estates, on the other hand, have a greater need for public recreational space.

Context beyond
the area of
investigation
When analyzing open space and green structure, the area of investigation's integration into its surroundings and into the city as a whole must be recorded. Of particular interest are the spatial connections between the individual green spaces and green infrastructure elements, and how the area of investigation's open spaces connect with their surroundings.

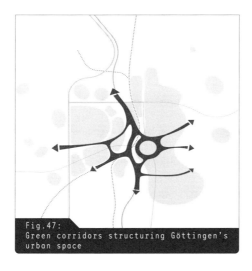

Fig.47:
Green corridors structuring Göttingen's urban space

Open space and green structure may have characteristic geometries, for instance a ring or central corridor system. These geometries often overlap – e.g. in a concentric open space system. › Fig. 47

Small connective elements and narrow green corridors may also be important in this context. Analyzing the integration situation also reveals whether open spaces outside the area of investigation are providing its residents with recreational space. The following are recorded:

_ The integration of housing into the landscape, connections between housing and open space, access to recreational spaces near housing
_ Green connective elements, e.g. avenues or grass verges
_ The interplay of open space and topography, e.g. green riverbanks or planted embankments
_ The spatial effect of green infrastructure elements, e.g. solitaires, rows or groups
_ Landscape profile, e.g. open or closed landscape

The qualities of many open space and green structures are only revealed in interaction. These networks are often incomplete, with gaps or spatial barriers. For purposes of general planning orientation, the connecting lines and corridors that only partially exist when the analysis is made should be recorded.

ANALYSIS OF CONSTRUCTION AND HOUSING STRUCTURE

Construction and housing structure analysis investigates the area of investigation's spatial composition, describing development characteristics and the construction development-open space relationship.

Recording
individual
features

Construction and housing analyses can be conducted to varying degrees of detail. For a plot-by-plot analysis, the structural features of every individual building are recorded based on a standardized catalogue and entered on a map. This degree of detail is necessary in urban analyses focusing on historically significant features, for which the following structural features might be recorded: › Fig. 48

_ Number of stories and building size (degree of construction saturation)
_ Building type (e.g. grouped houses, block, ribbon development)
_ Building form (e.g. closed or open building form)
_ Roof shape (e.g. pitched roof, hipped roof, flat roof)
_ Building orientation (e.g. with front or gable facing the street)
_ Access system (e.g. apartments with stairway access, block with outdoor-corridor access, block with inner access)
_ Added stylistic elements (e.g. ornamentation, beam decoration)
_ Building construction (e.g. solid construction or with a facade)
_ Age, construction era
_ Ownership situation (form of rental or ownership, diversified holdings or large-scale operator)

Granulation

The plot-by-plot analysis is used to identify subdivisions containing similar structural features, separating the area of investigation into sectors according to housing structure and original construction phase. This is generally done on the basis of building size and type and the age of the development. It is easiest to do this for areas with homogenous urban planning, i.e. subdivisions with unified development. Typical development structures include:

_ Closed block development
_ Open ribbon development
_ Compact ground-level construction
_ Freestanding apartment complex
_ Family home development

It is harder to differentiate areas with a non-uniform, apparently chaotic structure, which often make up most of the investigation area. In

Fig.48:
An individual building assessment often records the main facade's significant features.

this case, the degree of uniformity is used as the differentiating factor. Areas may, for instance, be listed as:

_ Compact block structure dating from the turn of the 20th century
_ Largely compact block structure from the turn of the 20th century, the 1950s and the 1960s
_ Open development structure with buildings from all periods

Construction and housing structure analysis often dispensed with this time-consuming individual assessment of buildings. In this case, subdivisions with similar housing structures are given at the outset. In a city with a mixed structure, this requires relevant practical knowledge.
> Fig. 49

\\ Note:
Further information on urban development types
is given in *Basics Urban Building Blocks* by
Thorsten Bürklin and Michael Peterek, Birkhäuser Verlag, Basel 2008.

Fig.49:
Identifying areas of specific ages and with specific housing structures

Urban spaces are created by the interaction of numerous buildings, or rather by the interaction of buildings with open spaces. These spaces have very different characteristics, e.g. › Figs 50 and 51

- _ Demarcation: spaces with closed or open character (clear demarcation or gradual transitions)
- _ Geometry: Spaces formed by geometrical edges (e.g. by building lines) or by irregularly positioned buildings
- _ Proportions: Relationship of buildings to open spaces, different densities and extents

Conversely, it is also necessary to identify imperfections and disruptions within the composition.

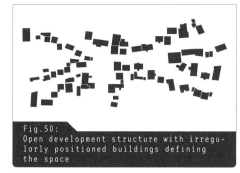

Fig.50:
Open development structure with irregularly positioned buildings defining the space

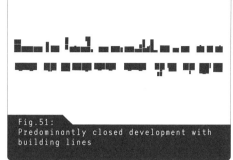

Fig.51:
Predominantly closed development with building lines

Context beyond the area of investigation

Construction and housing structures are usually influenced by spatial structures and structural elements that extend beyond the area of investigation. This often reveals the intrinsic logic of a housing structure and assists navigation within the city. Typical relationships include:

- _ Topography and housing structure: specific housing structures built on topographically different areas (e.g. large buildings on level ground, smaller-unit housing structures on less level ground)
- _ Orientation on a central space: certain housing characteristics increasing as a center is approached (e.g. increased housing density in the center of town relative to the periphery).

Exceptions to these rules are often described as disruptive, but may also be particularly exposed buildings or spatial elements that have important roles as landmarks.

Conclusion

Analyzing the construction and housing structure provides information on the function of the area of investigation. This can best be done by comparing the construction and housing structure analysis with the results of the land use structure analysis. A dense inner-city neighborhood with mixed land use structures generally takes on supply functions for other city neighborhoods. Due to their dense ground plan, however, these also place greater demand on public recreational spaces, which may need to be provided outside the area of investigation.

ANALYSIS OF SOCIAL SPACE

Social space analysis looks at the interaction of space with population structure, identifying urban areas within which population and spatial structure features are relatively constant. Social space analyses are

Fig.52:
Analyzing demographic features: the sizes of the statistical survey areas are based on neighborhoods.

generally conducted by social scientists, with urban analysts comparing the most important findings from their reports with other urban analysis results. This process creates insights useful to urban social planning, highlighting the spatial and topical key points for urban development and for the general social interest. › Fig. 52

Working methods   There are no universally established social space methods of analysis. Two different ways of posing the initial question, and two different working methods, are possible:

_ What is the spread of particular features of the population?
_ Which specific population features exist within a particular spatial area?

Referring to existing evaluations   In practice, city administrators continuously observe the population structure and its development within the boundaries of the city. As a rule, the individual statistical areas are based on administrative boundaries. An

Fig.53:
The area of investigation and the
statistical survey areas are generally
not identical in extent.

area of investigation for urban analysis, however, is generally not identical with an existing statistical area. Referring to existing observations will therefore produce only an inexact picture of the situation within the area of investigation. › Fig. 53 An analysis tailored to the area of investigation involves requesting data from the relevant census authority. This means that data availability, technical implementation, and data protection should be discussed at the outset.

Type and extent
of surveyed
characteristics

The simplest form of social analysis involves recording the population. By recording the population on a series of reference dates, population development can be recorded.

› 🗎

By calculating the number of inhabitants relative to spatial units, specific densities can be determined – the housing density (number of inhabitants per hectare of occupied space) or the occupancy rate (average number of residents per home).

🗎
\\ Note:
There are many possible evaluation methods for
surveying and evaluating population data (see
Appendix, Literature).

🗎
\\ Note:
Alongside population development, the influx
and exodus relative to the net population level
(fluctuation) can give a picture of an area of
investigation's population mobility.

A number of features of the area of investigation's population can be assessed, depending on the investigative approach and the capacity of the responsible census authority. Relevant population features might include age, sex, marital status, number of children, births, deaths, nationalities, arrivals and departures, and demand on welfare services. Spatial features might include the number and size of homes or the age of buildings.

Long-term analysis is needed to reveal developmental trends. These features should therefore be recorded on several separate reference dates.

Spatial
dimensions
of surveyed
features
The unequal distribution of various urban population groups is re-flected at the micro level in individual streets or building sites. If some parts of the investigated area have significantly different urban planning structures, a more fine-grained social space analysis will be needed to de-fine the interactions between social and spatial features. This means that two different approaches are possible:

1. To relate all features to the area of investigation as a unified sur-vey area and then compare the results with other survey areas.
2. To divide the area of investigation up spatially based on the sur-veyed features – i.e. to determine which features are present in which sections of the area of investigation.

› 🄊

Comparative
data
Comparing the situation within the area of investigation with other survey areas (e.g. the district, the whole city, the region) usually means acquiring data from higher-level institutions. When using different data sources, there is a risk that the recorded data were not collected using the same methods, thus making the comparison invalid.

🄊
\\ Note:
When referring to data from the responsible census authorities, the spatial area for which data on various features can be provided should be ascertained at the outset. Data protection for data on a small spatial area is particu-larly sensitive – the smaller the surveyed space, the greater the danger of surveyed fea-tures being traced back to individual people (see Fig. 54).

Fig.54:
Analyzing demographic features within a small area

Legend:
0-25%
>25-50%
>50-75%
>75-100%

Conclusion The survey will generally be used to draw conclusions about the social situation of people living in the area of investigation and the way the social situation there relates to the spatial surroundings. Reading straightforward meanings into the findings risks a false interpretation, as individual features provide limited material for substantiating such a conclusion. For instance, high population fluctuation may indicate low population stability and therefore the residents' low identification with their neighborhood. In the case of a neighborhood largely occupied by students, however, there would be nothing unusual about this. Any interpretation must therefore take into account a number of interacting features, and factor in the surveyed area's intended function. It is a particularly good idea to compare the results with those of the construction and housing structure analysis and the land use structure analysis. The expert knowledge of residents and people active in the area should also be incorporated.

> Chapter Working in the area under analysis

Social segregation, the spatial drifting apart of the population structure, runs contrary to the guiding principle of a socially mixed population
structure. Social differentiation, however, means that there will always be
neighborhoods with particular social milieus or classes, i.e. of people living similar lifestyles. This development is not necessarily problematic, as
social milieus can make access to certain social networks easier. The spatial concentration of social extremes, however, can create ghettoes, signal-
ing a mass presence of negative extremes in a single neighborhood and the
isolation of inhabitants from social services and modernization. Any social
space analysis must recognize these areas.

INTERPRETATION AND ILLUSTRATION

Initial evaluations are generally carried out for each sectoral analysis before considering the interactions between the different categories.

It is comparatively easy to evaluate an individual sectoral analysis, as comparisons can be made based on standardized values. An evaluation will usually be carried out under two headings: structure and function.

INTERACTION OF THE RESULTS OF SECTORAL ANALYSIS

A city, i.e. an entity perceived as a city is created by interacting spatial, functional and social factors. At the same time, too many competing claims on urban space are the cause of many urban dysfunctions and conflicts. Determining the difference between acceptable negative impact of one factor and another and actual conflict is an important part of urban analysis. It is not possible to record all the interactions, either for a whole city or for a single part of the city, and so the part of an urban analysis that deals with interactions, like the part that deals with sectoral factors, represents only an abstract model of the city.

Sectoral
analysis

Sectoral analysis evaluation generally follows a pattern of cause and effect: what is the cause of a spatial circumstance, and what are the consequences? Many evaluations, however, depend on the interactions between sectoral factors. For instance, a transport structure analysis may reveal that the capacity of a road needs to be increased. Once other factors have been taken into account – e.g. the location of the road within a residential area – it may not be possible to satisfy this requirement.

Comparing
sectoral
analyses

Certain needs and thereby the over- or under-provision of particular functions in the area of investigation can be determined by comparing sectoral analyses. This usually means including areas outside the area of investigation. Typical factors determining need are:

_ Development density and provision of recreational spaces
_ Population and provision of housing-associated facilities, e.g. facilities providing for everyday needs

CONCLUDING EVALUATION

Function of
the area of
investigation

The concluding evaluation must always refer back to the original starting point of the urban analysis. > Chapter Preparation and planning phases It must also either answer the original question or give a comprehensive picture of the situation within the area of investigation. Answering the original question does not usually mean questioning the area of investigation's function. Instead this function – the investigated area's role in the city's overall planning scheme – decides the appropriateness of any specific new development. Analysts determine appropriate land uses on this basis. If, on the other hand, the analysis presents the whole situation rather than starting with a specific issue, <u>strong points and opportunities</u> and <u>weak points and dangers</u> must be presented. In this case, a new function for the area of investigation may be suggested after appraising these factors. With both types of analysis, therefore, the investigated area's function must be taken into consideration. Function in this case means the main role of the area in the wider context of the city, on the basis of which it is evaluated. The area may for instance function as a purely residential district but also be capable of providing a supply function for the whole city, if properly equipped. Its function must be determined in the context of the whole city – i.e. the features of the area of investigation must be seen in relation to the structural features of the city as a whole.

In the part of the concluding analysis dealing with urban dysfunctions, the functional and substantial weaknesses of the area of investigation can be differentiated. A problem that prevents the area of investigation from fulfilling its function is a <u>functional weakness</u>. If a problem with the area of investigation's material make-up is detrimental to healthy living or working conditions, or endangers people living and working there,

Strengths	Weaknesses
- good access	- gaps in local
- plenty of	services
green space	- noise pressures
- cultural diversity	- vacancies
Opportunities	**Dangers**
- a place for young	- increase in
families to live	vacancies
- conversion of empty	- damage to local
buildings	image

Fig.55:
Arrangement of positive and negative
aspects in an evaluation matrix

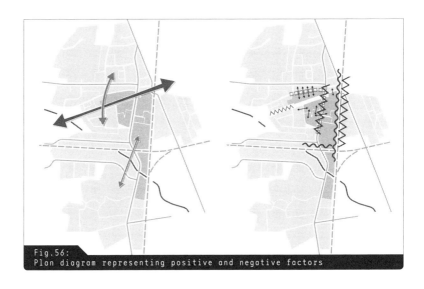

Fig.56:
Plan diagram representing positive and negative factors

this is a <u>substantial weakness</u>. Substantial weaknesses may apply only to parts of the area of investigation.

Assessing opportunities and dangers means looking beyond the status quo, using the analysis results to identify the area of investigation's possible future development. Analysts must base these theories closely on the area of investigation's spatial tendencies in particular. Opportunities might include, for instance, converting wasteland into public green space or using empty buildings for new forms of housing. Dangers might include a continuation of negative trends or committing urban planning errors.

Evaluation matrix and graphic plan representation

In practice, two methods are used to illustrate all these aspects:

1. Evaluation matrix representation, i.e. arranging positive and negative factors in a table. Aspects entered into the table can be placed in sequence to express their relative importance. > Fig. 55
2. A plan graphic representing positive and negative factors. This is particularly useful for showing the spatial relevance of all aspects. > Fig. 56

TRANSITION TO SUBSEQUENT COURSE OF ACTION

If an urban analysis gives an overall picture of the area of investigation, then weighing up all analysis results will form the basis for a future development reference model. As rigid plans of action often cannot be implemented in practice due to the many circumstances beyond planners' control, the following approach is advisable:

1. Establish a development model for the area of investigation
2. Sketch out several alternative action plans or development scenarios

Reference model   As a strategic overall goal, the reference model provides orientation for any future development steps. Any feasible individual measures or packages of measures can be realized without losing sight of this model, which is developed from analysis results according to three sets of rules:
> Fig. 57

_ Descriptive or analytical: identifying future developments based on researched trends
_ Goal-oriented or normative: determining required actions based on desired goals
_ Initial or investigative: investigating factors likely to give impetus to future developments

The goals envisaged by urban analysis can influence the area of investigation's development in three different ways:

1. Active and activating effect:
_ Project preparation, e.g. a feasibility study
_ Translation into an action plan or contingency plan
_ Identifying areas of potential
_ Acquiring financial support

2. Controlling effect:
_ Laying down rules for the event of a project's being carried out
_ "If ... then" options

3. Conservative or passive effect:
_ Preventing undesirable developments
_ Safeguarding existing areas of potential

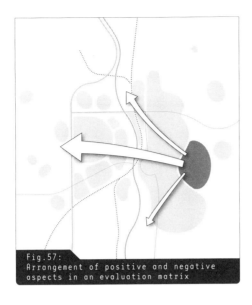

Fig.57:
Arrangement of positive and negative
aspects in an evaluation matrix

ILLUSTRATION OF THE RESULTS OF ANALYSIS

Representation
using maps

Where possible, evaluations and interpretations should be displayed in graphic plans as well as textually, in order to clarify the different aspects' spatial applications. All analysis results are entered on scale maps and given values, identified in a key. Depending on the degree of detail, it may be a good idea to divide the recorded characteristics into headings and subheadings. The key should be structured to reflect this division, with all the subcategories for a particular heading given a single color – shades of red, for instance. Representations in the plan and on the map will be based on a standardized key. Depending on the type of representation required, the outlines of buildings, plots or building sites will be used. › Fig. 58

While formal planning texts contain clear instructions for using plan symbols, urban analysis has no plan symbol standards. Preparing easily readable graphic representations of analysis results is an important part of urban analysis.

Representation-
al scale

The correct scale for representing analysis results on a map must be chosen according to the size of the area of investigation and the degree of detail in the analysis. The decisive factor here is which urban space element represents the smallest determining unit, i.e. spatial unit.

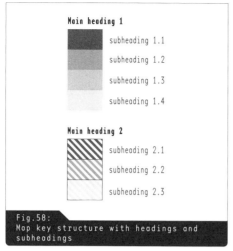

Main heading 1
subheading 1.1
subheading 1.2
subheading 1.3
subheading 1.4

Main heading 2
subheading 2.1
subheading 2.2
subheading 2.3

Fig.58:
Map key structure with headings and subheadings

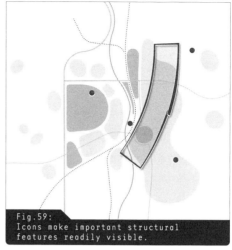

Fig.59:
Icons make important structural features readily visible.

For <u>whole-city analyses</u>, the smallest spatial unit is generally the building site or neighborhood. Scales of between 1:20,000 and 1:5000 are used. A topographical map is likely to be used as the basis.

<u>District-level investigations</u> generally include information on individual buildings or plots. A suitable scale is 1:2000 or 1:1000. A real estate map is likely to be used as the basis.

<u>Small-area investigations</u> (e.g. individual building plots or streets) are represented on maps using scales of 1:500 to 1:200.

Sketches and icons

Abstract sketches and icons are suitable for illustrating the most important interpretation points. Reducing these to their significant structural features enables a plastic approach to these interpretations and the spaces to which they apply. › Fig. 59

Representing statistical analyses

Statistical analyses can be applied to the area of investigation as a unified whole, be used to compare the area of investigation as a whole with other census areas or make statements about individual areas within the area of investigation.

Spreadsheet programs are generally used to process statistical data. These programs contain tools for representing the statistics as diagrams. If the area of investigation is being evaluated only as a statistical survey area, these tools will generally be sufficient to illustrate the evaluations.

Fig.60:
Spatially relevant statistical analysis

If the area of investigation is being minutely investigated and divided into several census areas, maps showing these census areas will be needed. These evaluations are usually organized in a table of values and entered on a map according to a standardized key. › Fig. 60

Fig.61:
Deviations in perception of the area of investigation have to be taken into account in any urban analysis.

IN CONCLUSION

Urban analyses are not the sum of several individual analyses. Instead, they integrate several analyses into a single picture. The quality of an urban analysis is determined by awareness of any specific area of investigation's different interacting aspects, rather than detailed listing of the individual sectoral factors. The overall picture can only be seen when the interactions between the various sectoral factors are taken into account, and this is what ultimately determines accuracy in an urban analysis.

Extensive collecting of data on individual factors can obscure the interactions. Sectoral analyses should therefore be conducted with a view to the degree of detail the concluding evaluation will be able to handle. Digitizing spatial and population-related data has made a large amount of data comparatively quick to obtain. To prevent large, incoherent collections of data, these data must be checked for relevance prior to incorporation into the evaluation – a task requiring experience and an awareness of its specific purposes and goals.

Urban analyses create an abstract, model representation of an urban reality to serve as a basis for future urban planning measures in the area of investigation. However, as urban analyses cannot satisfactorily research certain aspects, such as emotional ties and social habits, they often contradict the perceptions of involved parties – an unavoidable fact that should be taken into account by anyone acting on the basis of an urban analysis.

Urban analyses that consult residents' wishes are the cornerstone of successful cooperations between residents, authorities, and other participants in urban life. Against a background of urban development within existing urban structures becoming more frequent, this kind of urban analysis can be a vital part of sustainable urban development.

APPENDIX

LITERATURE

Christopher Alexander, Sara Ishikawa, Murray Silverstein: *A Pattern Language: Towns, Buildings, Construction*, Oxford University Press, 1978

Carl Fingerhuth: *Learning from China. The Tao of the City*, Birkhäuser Verlag, Basel 2004

Peter Hall: *Urban and Regional Planning*, Taylor & Francis, 2002

Kevin Lynch: *The Image of the City*, MIT Press, 1960

Franz Oswald, Peter Baccini: *Netzstadt. Designing the Urban*, Birkhäuser Verlag, Basel 2003

Colin Rowe: *Collage City*, MIT Press, 1984

Aldo Rossi: *The Architecture of the City*, MIT Press, 1984

Thomas Sieverts: *Cities Without Cities. Between Place and World, Space and Time, Town and Country*, Routledge Chapman & Hall, London New York 2003

PICTURE CREDITS

Figure 7:	© kittel+partner, Dresden. Shows: Peek&Cloppenburg department store in the centre of Chemnitz
Figure 9 (left):	Graphic: G. Schwalbach. Source: The city of Göttingen in the Middle Ages, Map 2 from O. Fahlbusch: "Die Topografie der Stadt Göttingen", Göttingen 1962
Figure 9 (center):	G. Schwalbach. Source: GOETTINGA, urbs munitissima et splendida ..., an urban plan by Matthias Seutter, Augsburg (copper engraving from around 1750). Graphic design: Atelier K.-H. Fehrecke, commissioned by city of Göttingen construction authority, first published in 1971
Figure 9 (right):	Graphic: G. Schwalbach. Source: plan by municipal planning office of Göttingen 1893. Graphic design: Atelier K.-H. Fehrecke, commissioned by city of Göttingen construction authority. First published in 1971
Figures 10, 48:	Pesch & Partner: Architekten+Stadtplaner, Herdecke/Stuttgart: Gestaltungsfibel und -satzung Innenstadt Coesfeld (design manual and design statutes for inner-city Coesfeld), Herdecke 2006
Figures 19, 21:	© Geobasisdaten (spatial base data) Bundesland North Rhine-Westphalia, Bonn

THE AUTHOR

Gerrit Schwalbach, Dipl.-Ing. architect, research assistant in urban planning and history of planning in the Department of Architecture and Urban Planning at the University of Siegen, Germany

Series editor: Bert Bielefeld
Conception: Bert Bielefeld, Annette Gref
Layout and cover design: Muriel Comby
Translation into English: Michael Robinson
English copy editing: Monica Buckland

Library of Congress Control Number: 2009928654

Bibliographic information published by the
German National Library
The German National Library lists this publication in the Deutsche Nationalbibliografie; detailed bibliographic data are available on the Internet at http://dnb.d-nb.de.

This book is also available in a German language edition (ISBN 978-3-7643-8937-6).

© 2009 Birkhäuser Verlag AG
Basel · Boston · Berlin
P.O. Box 133, CH-4010 Basel, Switzerland
Part of Springer Science+Business Media

Printed on acid-free paper produced from chlorine-free pulp. TCF ∞
Printed in Germany

ISBN 978-3-7643-8938-3

9 8 7 6 5 4 3 2 1   www.birkhauser.ch

Also available from Birkhäuser:

Design
Basics Barrier-free Planning
Isabella Skiba, Rahel Züger
ISBN 978-3-7643-8958-1

Basics Design and Living
Jan Krebs
978-3-7643-7647-5

Basics Design Ideas
Bert Bielefeld, Sebastian El khouli
978-3-7643-8112-7

Basics Design Methods
Kari Jormakka
978-3-7643-8463-0

Basics Materials
M. Hegger, H. Drexler, M. Zeumer
978-3-7643-7685-7

Basics Spatial Design
Ulrich Exner, Dietrich Pressel
978-3-7643-8848-5

Fundamentals of Presentation
Basics Architectural Photography
Michael Heinrich
978-3-7643-8666-5

Basics CAD
Jan Krebs
978-3-7643-8109-7

Basics Modelbuilding
Alexander Schilling
978-3-7643-7649-9

Basics Technical Drawing
Bert Bielefeld, Isabella Skiba
978-3-7643-7644-4

Construction
Basics Facade Apertures
Roland Krippner, Florian Musso
978-3-7643-8466-1

Basics Glass Construction
Andreas Achilles, Diane Navratil
978-3-7643-8851-5

Basics Loadbearing Systems
Alfred Meistermann
978-3-7643-8107-3

Basics Masonry Construction
Nils Kummer
978-3-7643-7645-1

Basics Roof Construction
Tanja Brotrück
978-3-7643-7683-3

Basics Timber Construction
Ludwig Steiger
978-3-7643-8102-8

Building Services / Building Physics
Basics Room Conditioning
Oliver Klein, Jörg Schlenger
978-3-7643-8664-1

Basics Water Cycles
Doris Haas-Arndt
978-3-7643-8854-6

Professional Practice
Basics Construction Scheduling
Bert Bielefeld
978-3-7643-8873-7

Basics Project Planning
Hartmut Klein
978-3-7643-8469-2

Basics Site Management
Lars-Phillip Rusch
978-3-7643-8104-2

Basics Tendering
Tim Brandt, Sebastian Th. Franssen
978-3-7643-8110-3

Urbanism
Basics Urban Building Blocks
Thorsten Bürklin, Michael Peterek
978-3-7643-8460-9

Landscape Architecture
Basics Designing with Plants
Regine Ellen Wöhrle, Hans-Jörg Wöhrle
978-3-7643-8659-7

Basics Designing with Water
Axel Lohrer
978-3-7643-8662-7

BIRKHÄUSER

Available from your bookshop or at www.birkhauser.ch